an Affair to Remember

★ State Dinners for Home Entertaining ★

Laurie G. Firestone
Former White House Social Secretary

Introduction

Nothing is more exciting than being invited to the White House for a formal dinner. I remember my first dinner, when Richard Nixon was President very well. My husband and I were invited to honor Ray Bliss, the retiring Chairman of the Republican National Committee. It was a wonderful event, with beautiful flowers everywhere. The United States Marine Corps Orchestra played throughout the evening, and a delicious four-course dinner was accompanied by three excellent wines. To my delight, I was seated at the President's table and even had the nerve to ask him for his autograph during dessert—which he graciously signed. It was a magical evening!

I never imagined that, years later, I would become the White House Social Secretary to President George H.W. Bush and First Lady, Barbara Bush. In that capacity, I wanted to help create the same atmosphere and magical feeling for everyone who attended a White House event—so that they, too, would have an experience of a lifetime. It was a tremendously challenging and fun position and involved a great deal of management and organization.

The President and First Lady loved to entertain, hosting an astonishing 40,000 people annually. If there was ever a free day or evening on the calendar, they would host a last-minute buffet dinner and movie, or barbeque and horseshoes.

President Bush placed great importance on his personal relationships with friends and world leaders, and frequent entertaining was one of the ways he maintained those relationships. He felt that negotiations often were more successful if the individuals involved had an opportunity to "break bread" together in a friendly social atmosphere before a meeting.

While all of the entertaining at the White House was exciting, the most glamorous events were the Official State Visits and accompanying formal State Dinners. The White House hosts only a few State Visits each year, making them a most coveted invitation by foreign dignitaries, celebrities, and members of the press. Visits usually last for three days, and are comprised of a formal arrival ceremony for the foreign Head of State on the South Lawn, official meetings, and, of course, a formal State Dinner in the State Dining Room. These dinners are an invaluable opportunity for the President, First Lady, and administration officials to sit down in a social setting with foreign leaders, lending a personal aspect to politics and allowing both parties to forge genuine relationships.

The White House has long recognized the importance of entertaining politicians and notable figures in a setting where individuals of divergent opinions feel welcome and comfortable. Dolly Madison, wife of President James Madison, established Wednesday Drawing Rooms. These gatherings often had as many as 200 guests for an evening of food, conversation, and whiskey punch. Mrs. Madison did not send formal invitations to these affairs and as a result, political rivals often found themselves together by chance, while decorum required them to socialize. These spontaneous events amused Washington high society, and facilitated communication between opposing parties and created a sense of unity in the newly formed government.

The White House has been hosting State Dinners since its construction in 1801, although the State Dining Room was not officially used for that purpose until Andrew Jackson's administration when the nearby stables were moved to another part of the house. The tradition of formal guest reception, dinner, and after-dinner entertainment, however, was not conceived until 1898, when the Lent ensemble played for President and Mrs. McKinley and seventy guests after a lavish dinner for the Supreme Court. That enchanting night set the stage for the dinner/musical as the focal point for entertaining at the White House, and this format remains today.

The State Dining Room, which now seats as many as 130 guests, was originally much smaller and served at various times as a drawing room, office, and Cabinet Room. Not until Andrew Jackson's administration was it called the "State Dining Room," although it had been used for formal dinners by previous Presidents.

For years, the State Dinner took place at a large U-shaped table in the State Dining Room. During the Kennedy administration, at Mrs. Kennedy's request, State Dinners changed from one large table to multiple circular tables with colored cloths, facilitating more free-flowing and engaging conversation.

Planning for a State Dinner begins months in advance between the emissaries of the two governments, but the final stage of completing the arrangements occurs several weeks before the actual event. First, and most importantly, the White House Executive Chef and Social Secretary discuss the menu. State Dinners generally include four courses, including dessert. At this critical stage, many factors are addressed, including dietary or religious restrictions, cultural expectations, and personal likes or dislikes. The President himself may even weigh in with his own choices!

After deciding on a menu with the Chef, the Social Secretary presents it to the First Lady for her approval. Many First Ladies, including Mrs. Bush, have taken an active role in planning State Dinners and become involved not just in the menus, but in other details such as the selection of entertainment, flower arrangements, tablecloths, and wine.

On the day of a State Dinner, the White House is a flurry of activity, with staff busy setting up tables, ironing table-cloths, arranging centerpieces, and finishing the elegant, calligraphic place cards and table cards for each guest. Each Presidential administration has its own official set of china, many of which are still used in the White House today and reflect the changing aesthetic tastes of America. Sadly, some of these sets have shrunk over the years due to loss and breakage. Many feature unique patriotic themes such as American wildflowers as with the Johnson china. Others are simple and elegant, such as the Regan china which is edged in red and gold. Which ever china is used, it is set off beautifully by flatware, crystal, and centerpieces.

In the kitchen, the White House Chef and Sous Chefs are busy with the task of creating world-class fare. And, in her office, the White House Social Secretary begins the delicate and subtly difficult task of arranging the seating chart for the evening.

The arrangement of guests at a State Dinner is as important as the guests themselves, and must take into account basic political, cultural, and ideological differences. Guest lists normally include a group suggested by the State Department's Protocol Office, and a group suggested by the foreign and domestic offices of the President. The Foreign Leader's Party usually numbers around 15 people. Also included are representatives from the Senate, Congress, Supreme Court, Cabinet, press, and business leaders. Spouses and fiancés are always invited.

With so many guests attending each State Dinner, supplemental staff is hired to help for the evening. In addition to the chefs, florists, calligraphers, advisors, and staff already mentioned, the White House waiters and Social Aides deserve special recognition. The waiters take great pride in their work; some have served at the White House for as long as 40 years—through eight or nine administrations.

The Social Aides assist the White House Social Secretary in greeting guests as they arrive. These men and women are junior commissioned officers in the United States Military, representing all 5 services with ranks between Second Lieutenant and Major.

The evening begins promptly at 7:30 PM. Guests are given their table cards and escorted by one of the Social Aides into the East Room for cocktails. At the same time, the President and First Lady go to the North Portico to greet the motorcade of the visiting Head of State. The honorees are taken upstairs to the Yellow Oval Room for a brief visit. Joining them upstairs is the Vice President and his wife, the Secretary of State and his wife and the Chief of Protocol.

Approximately 20 minutes later, the President and First Lady escort the visiting Head of State and spouse down the Grand Stairway with the honor guard leading the way and the Marine Corps Orchestra playing "Hail to the Chief". At the bottom of the Grand Stairway, pictures are taken, and then the group moves into the East Room for a receiving line. After being greeted, the guests stroll down the Cross Hall, to the music of the Marine Orchestra, and into the State Dining Room where they find their places at the table. Waiters stand attentively at the doors to assist guests who need help finding their seats.

Once the guests are seated, toasts are exchanged. Toasts are held before dinner, and then members of the press leave the dining room. Following the toast, dinner is French service— whereby the waiters pass the food on platters for the guests to serve themselves. Domestic wines from all over the United States are served.

Dinner lasts just over an hour. As dessert is being served, the Army Strolling Strings serenade the guests. When everyone is finished, the President and First Lady lead their guests into the Blue Room, where after-dinner coffee is offered.

While the guests have been eating dinner, the staff has been busy setting up chairs, theater style, in the East Room. The entertainment which follows State Dinners is always exceptional. The White House has attracted many of the greatest artists of our time—Leontine Price, Jessye Norman, Yo Yo Ma, and Isaac Stern, to name a few.

Following the entertainment, the President and First Lady say their good-byes to the honorees and escort them to the North Portico, where they are met by a motorcade and taken back to Blair House, the formal guest house for Presidential visitors.

At this point, the night is generally far from over. There is still dancing and champagne—sometimes to the disappointment of the foreign Heads of State! The President and First Lady go upstairs after a few dances, and the evening usually ends by midnight.

My goal in writing this book is twofold: first, to share my remarkable experience as a very fortunate eyewitness to the unfolding of American history; and second, to provide an accessible home entertaining book that captures the spirit of State Dinners so that you can make your own events even more memorable. Throughout this book, in addition to photographs from my personal archive and many memorable anecdotes, you will find a collection of some of my favorite State Dinner menus, with images of the actual Menu Card that each guest was given at their place setting. In deciding which recipes to include, after realizing that most of them require too much prep time or are too complicated for typical home entertaining, working with food editors and chefs, I've come up with simplified versions for many of these outstanding dishes. For those of you who are more

daring with your culinary skills, I have included a few original recipes from Hans Raffert, the former White House Executive Chef. Hans served at the White House for five Presidents—12 years as Executive Sous Chef and 11 years as Executive Chef.

The years I worked in the White House are some of my fondest memories. We strived, and succeeded, in making every guest feel like a Head of State. In creating your own memorable experiences, whether simple or formal, I encourage you to keep your focus on making your guests feel special. Then you, too, will create some memories of a lifetime.

April 6, 1989

DINNER

Honoring
His Excellency
The Prime Minister of Israel
and Mrs. Shamir

Supreme of Smoked Trout
Horseradish Sauce
Herbed Bow Ties

Breast of Chicken Rosemary
with Wild Mushrooms
Rice Pilaf Valencienne
Turban of Spinach

Watercress and Belgian Endive Salad
St. André Cheese

Strawberry Sorbet Bombe
Cookies

HAGAFEN *Johannisberg Riesling* 1988
HAGAFEN *Chardonnay* 1988
DOMAINE CHANDON *Blanc de Noirs*

THE WHITE HOUSE
Thursday, April 6, 1989

Guests sit down for an elegant State Dinner in the State Dinner dining room.

The Social Aides, who assisted my staff, were commissioned officers in the United States military, representing all 5 services. They are junior officers with ranks between a 2nd lieutenant and a major. Standing with me in this picture were all the aides, Cathy Fenton, my deputy assistant, and Bobby Chung, head of the military office.

Breast of Chicken Rosemary with Wild Mushrooms

Serves 4

Rinse chicken, pat dry, and season with salt and pepper. In a small bowl, whisk together wine and rosemary, cover, and set aside.

Heat oil and butter in a skillet then add onions and sauté 2–3 minutes. Add chicken and brown over medium low heat, 2–3 minutes on each side. Add wine, cover, and lightly simmer for 30 minutes. Add mushrooms and continue to simmer, covered for 10 more minutes, until chicken is thoroughly cooked.

Arrange chicken and mushrooms on plates and drizzle rosemary wine sauce over the top.

3 lbs boneless chicken breasts

⅓ cup dry white wine

2 tsp fresh rosemary, chopped

1 tbs olive oil

1 tbs unsalted butter

2 tbs onion, chopped

8 oz assorted wild mushrooms

Kosher salt

Freshly ground black pepper

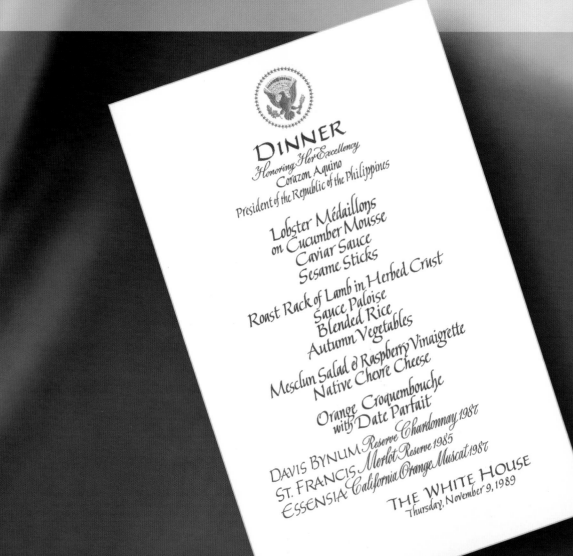

DINNER
Honoring Her Excellency
Corazon Aquino
President of the Republic of the Philippines

Lobster Médaillons
on Cucumber Mousse
Caviar Sauce
Sesame Sticks

Roast Rack of Lamb in Herbed Crust
Sauce Paloise
Blended Rice
Autumn Vegetables

Mesclun Salad & Raspberry Vinaigrette
Native Chèvre Cheese

Orange Croquembouche
with Date Parfait

DAVIS BYNUM Reserve Chardonnay 1987
ST. FRANCIS Merlot Reserve 1985
ESSENSIA California Orange Muscat 1987

THE WHITE HOUSE
Thursday, November 9, 1989

At this State Dinner in honor of President Corazon Aquino of the Philippines, the beautiful Reagan china —red, white, and gold—was used. What made this a very memorable evening was that President Bush, after being given a message from his aide, stood and announced that the Berlin Wall had finally fallen. The guests were at first stunned and then broke into wild applause. Sitting on the President's left was Dena Merrill.

Christmas was truly a magical time at the White House. The State Dinner with President Aquino was the closest to Christmas this year. It took months of advance preparation and four days to decorate the house, with the help of 40 volunteers.

Roast Rack of Lamb in Herbed Crust

Serves 4

Preheat to 400°F.

Remove lamb from refrigerator and bring to room temperature; season with salt and pepper.

In a small bowl, combine breadcrumbs, rosemary, parsley, and mint and season with a little salt and pepper. Add 1 tablespoon olive oil and stir until combined.

Heat remaining olive oil in a heavy skillet over medium high heat until hot but not smoking. Brown lamb, beginning with fat side facing up for 2 minutes. Turn, and brown other side for 2 more minutes. Transfer to a roasting pan, fat side facing up.

Baste top of lamb with mustard then spread breadcrumb mixture, gently pressing to adhere. Roast for 20–25 minutes on middle oven rack or until a meat thermometer registers 130°F (for medium-rare). Transfer to a cutting board, let rest for 10 minutes, then cut into chops and serve.

3 lb rack of lamb (4-ribs), trimmed of all but a thin layer of fat

¾ cup breadcrumbs

1 tsp fresh rosemary, chopped

2 tbs fresh Italian parsley, chopped

½ tbs fresh mint, chopped

2 tbs extra virgin olive oil, separated

1 tbs Dijon mustard

Kosher salt

Freshly ground black pepper

Mesclun Salad & Raspberry Vinaigrette

Serves 4

Thoroughly rinse greens and dry.

In a small bowl, whisk together vinegars, mustard, shallots, and sugar. Slowly whisk in olive oil to emulsify, and season with salt and pepper, adding additional sugar to taste if necessary.

Toss greens with dressing and arrange on salad plates. Garnish with raspberries.

1 lb mixed spring greens

1 tbs Champagne vinegar

2 tbs raspberry vinegar

½ tsp Dijon mustard

2 large shallots, diced

1 tsp sugar

½ cup extra virgin olive oil

Kosher salt

Freshly ground black pepper

Raspberries for garnish

February 12, 1990

DINNER

Honoring His Excellency
The President of the Peoples Republic of the Congo
and Mrs. Sassou-Nguesso

Mousse of Salmon
Caviar Sauce
Sesame Sticks

Loin of Lamb Farci Chartreuse
Morel Sauce
Saffron Rice & Vegetable Timbale
Asparagus & Baby Carrots

Mesclun Salad
Avocado Oil Dressing
Saint Paulin Cheese

Biscuit Turinois
with Caramel Sauce

TALBOTT Chardonnay 1987
JORDAN Cabernet Sauvignon 1985
FIRESTONE Johannisberg Riesling Select Harvest 1986

THE WHITE HOUSE
Monday, February 12, 1990

Once guests were seated for dinner, toasts were exchanged so the press could leave for the evening. The Bushes preferred to have toasts before, rather than after dinner.

President Teddy Roosevelt purchased this chandelier for the dining room in 1902 in New York City. In 1961 Mrs. Kennedy had it re-finished in gold-plated bronze dorie.

You might also notice the ornate eagle lectern, which the President and his guests always used. Interpreters (if needed) had their own podium and microphone in the far-left corner of the room.

Mousse of Salmon

Serves 4

Preheat oven to 400°F.

Rinse salmon, pat dry, and season with olive oil, salt, and pepper. Place on a baking sheet and bake for 10 to 12 minutes. Remove from oven, cool completely, and chill in refrigerator for at least 30 minutes.

While salmon is chilling; combine mayonnaise, onion, lemon juice, Tabasco, paprika, and dill by hand or in a food processor and season with salt. Remove salmon from refrigerator and slice into small pieces. Fold into mousse and chill for 30 more minutes.

Rinse cucumber and slice into 8—½ inch rounds. Arrange a dollop of mousse on top of each cucumber slice with caviar on top and garnish with dill sprigs.

1 lb salmon fillet, skin and pin bones removed

1 tsp extra virgin olive oil

½ cup mayonnaise

1 tbs red onion, diced

1 tbs fresh lemon juice

Dash of Tabasco®

¼ tsp Hungarian sweet paprika

2 tbs fresh dill, chopped

1 cucumber

1 oz caviar

Dill sprigs

Kosher or sea salt

Freshly ground black pepper

Loin of Lamb Farci Chartreuse

Serves 6

Preheat oven to 375°F.

Rinse lamb and pat dry. In a small bowl, combine 1 tablespoon olive oil and rosemary. Set aside.

Melt butter and remaining olive oil in a heavy skillet over medium high heat. Add leeks, garlic, and cabbage and sauté until cabbage is tender, about 6 minutes.

Open lamb like book with cut side facing up. Season with salt and pepper and spread cabbage filling evenly. Roll tightly, enclosing the filling. Rub outside with olive oil and rosemary mixture, and season with salt and pepper. Wrap bacon around lamb and tie with kitchen string at 2-inch intervals. Place on a rack in a roasting pan.

Roast in the oven until thermometer inserted into thickest part of lamb registers 135°F to 140°F for medium-rare, about 1 hour 25 minutes, then remove, cover with foil, and let rest for 15 minutes before removing string to slice.

4 lb lamb loin, trimmed and butterflied

2 tbs extra virgin olive oil, separated

1 tbs fresh rosemary, chopped

1 tbs butter

1 cup leeks, white parts sliced into rings

1 garlic clove, minced

1 cup Napa cabbage, chopped

8–10 strips bacon or pancetta

Rosemary sprigs

Kosher salt

Freshly ground black pepper

DINNER

Honoring
The Governors of the States and Territories

Baby Lobster American
Cucumber Sauce
Herbed Fleurons

Roasted Contre-Filet of Beef
Rissole Potatoes
Béarnaise Sauce
Almond Carrot Ring with Snow Peas

Boston Lettuce & Radish Julienne
Lemon-Yogurt Dressing
Native Chèvre Cheese

Strawberry Surprise - Melba Sauce
Cookies

Ferrari-Carano Chardonnay 1987
Château Ste. Michelle Merlot River Ridge Vineyard 1985
Domaine Chandon Blanc de Noirs

THE WHITE HOUSE
Sunday, February 25, 1990

This festive State Dinner was
in the Rose Garden.
The setting was magical
with thousands of white lights
illuminating the trees.

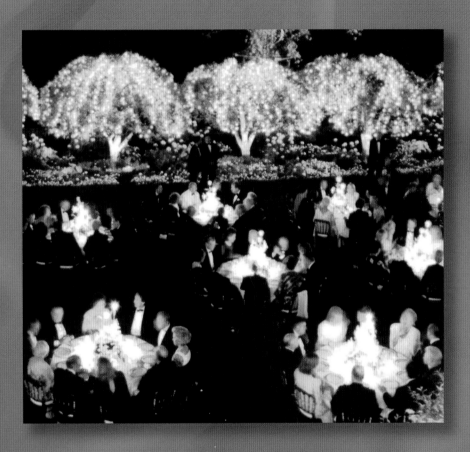

Roasted Contre-Filet of Beef

Serves 12

Rinse beef, pat dry, and season with salt and pepper.

Drop garlic into a running food processor and blend until finely chopped. Add sage, thyme, breadcrumbs, olive oil, and Worcestershire sauce and process until a paste forms. Rub paste thoroughly into beef then cover and refrigerate over night.

The following day, remove beef from refrigerator and preheat oven to 450°F.

Place beef fat side up on roasting pan rack. Roast for 15 minutes, then reduce oven temperature to 350°F and roast for 35 more minutes for medium-rare (until thermometer inserted into thickest part registers 130°F), or 40 minutes for medium (140°F).

Remove from oven and let rest for 20 minutes. Cut crosswise, arrange slices on platter, and drizzle with Béarnaise Sauce.

7 lb boneless beef loin

6 garlic cloves, peeled

12 fresh sage leaves

2 tbs fresh thyme sprigs, leaves removed

½ cup breadcrumbs

2 tbs extra virgin olive oil

1 tbs Worcestershire sauce

Kosher salt

Freshly ground black pepper

Béarnaise Sauce

In small saucepan, combine vinegar, wine, tarragon, chervil, peppercorns, and shallot. Bring to a boil over medium heat then reduce heat and simmer, uncovered, 8–10 minutes, until reduced to ¼ cup.

Heat water in a double boiler until hot, but not boiling. Pour sauce through a fine strainer into top of double boiler. With wire whisk, beat in egg yolks, beating constantly until sauce begins to thicken. Add butter, 1 tablespoon at a time, beating well after each addition until melted.

Keep sauce warm until ready to serve.

½ cup white vinegar

½ cup dry white wine

2 tbs fresh tarragon, chopped

1 tbs fresh chervil, chopped

4 peppercorns, crushed

2 tbs shallots, minced

6 egg yolks

1 cup unsalted butter

Rissole Potatoes

Serves 12

Preheat oven to 350°F.

In a large bowl, combine potatoes, onions, and garlic; drizzle with olive oil, toss until thoroughly coated, and season with salt and pepper. Transfer to a casserole dish with a cover and add stock. Place butter pieces on top of potatoes and cover. Bake for 25 minutes, then uncover and bake for 30 more minutes until browned, turning several times.

Remove potatoes from oven and garnish with parsley.

24 small whole baby red or fingerling potatoes

24 pearl onions, peeled

1 cup yellow onion, chopped

3 garlic cloves, minced

½ cup extra virgin olive oil

⅔ cup chicken stock

½ cup unsalted butter, cut into small pieces

Kosher salt

Freshly ground black pepper

½ cup fresh Italian parsley, chopped

March 2, 1990

DINNER

*Honoring His Excellency
The Prime Minister of Japan*

Salmon/Sole Mousseline
Smoked Salmon
Cucumbers

Beef Wellington
Glazed Carrots
Celeriac Purée
Haricots Verts

Soufflé Glacé Surprise
Vanilla-Chocolate Sauce
Petits Fours

ROBERT MONDAVI Chenin Blanc 1987
ROBERT MONDAVI Cabernet Sauvignon Reserve Mag 1974
SCHRAMSBERG Blanc de Noirs 1983

Friday, March 2, 1990

Yo Yo Ma entertaining at a State Dinner. We had the greatest artists of our time —Jessye Norman, Leontine Price, and Isaac Stern to name just a few.

Beef Wellington

Serves 8

Preheat oven to 350°F.

Rinse beef, pat dry, season with salt and pepper, and place in a roasting pan. Roast for 25–30 minutes on middle oven rack, or until meat thermometer registers 120°F. Remove, and cool completely.

In a heavy skillet, melt butter and sauté mushrooms over medium low heat, stirring, until all liquid evaporates and mixture is dry; season with salt and pepper, and cool completely.

Spread pâté de foie gras evenly over beef, covering top and sides, then spread mushrooms evenly over pâté.

Sprinkle a little flour over a work surface and roll puff pastry dough into a rectangle large enough to completely enclose beef. Place beef in the middle of pastry, fold up long sides to enclose, brushing edges with egg white to seal. Fold ends of pastry over beef and seal with remaining egg white.

Transfer, seam side down, to roasting pan and baste thoroughly with egg yolk. Place in refrigerator and chill for at least 1 hour.

Preheat oven to 400°F.

Remove from refrigerator and roast for 30 minutes on middle oven rack, reduce heat to 350°, and roast 5–10 minutes more, until meat thermometer registers 130°F for medium-rare and pastry is golden brown. Remove, and let rest for 15 minutes before slicing.

4 lb beef tenderloin

2 tbs unsalted butter

12 oz wild mushrooms, finely chopped (porcini, morel, shitake, etc.)

8 oz pâté de foie gras, at room temperature

16 oz puff pastry dough

1 large egg white, beaten

1 large egg yolk, beaten with 1 tsp of water

Flour for rolling out puff pastry

Kosher salt

Freshly ground black pepper

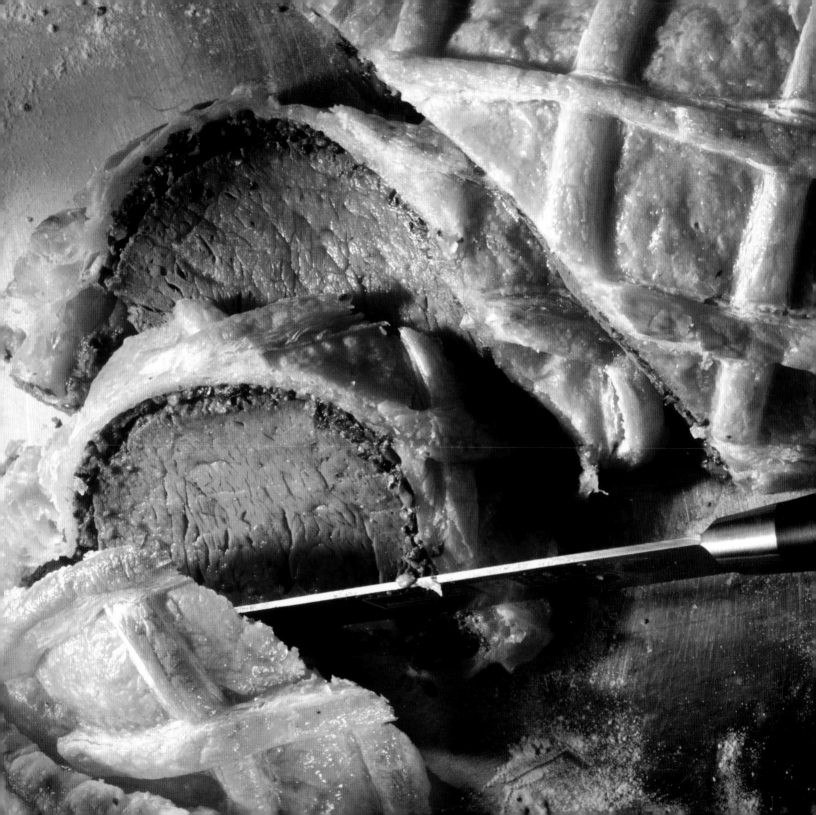

Glazed Carrots

Serves 8

In a deep, heavy skillet, bring stock, corn syrup, sugar, cream, and butter to a boil. Add carrots and cook until tender, but slightly crisp, about 5–6 minutes. Remove carrots with a slotted spoon and set aside. Boil remaining liquid until reduced to 1 cup, stirring frequently, then return carrots to skillet, stir in ginger and parsley, and season with salt and pepper.

2 cups vegetable stock

½ cup corn syrup

½ cup brown sugar, packed

½ cup heavy cream

2 tbs unsalted butter

2 lbs baby carrots, peeled

½ tsp fresh ginger, grated

¼ cup fresh Italian parsley, chopped

Kosher salt

Freshly ground pepper

Salmon/Sole Mousseline

Serves 8

Butter 8 (6 oz) ramekins with softened butter, place inside a large roasting pan, and set aside.

In a food processor, purée sole and salmon on high speed then add shallots, chives, parsley, dill, and pepper continuing to process on high until combined.

While processor is running, add egg whites and process thoroughly, then add melted butter, season with salt, and gradually add cream. Continue to purée on high, scraping sides several times. Transfer to a bowl, cover, and refrigerate until very cold, at least 1 hour.

Preheat oven to 350°F.

Divide mousse among prepared ramekins and fill roasting pan with water halfway up ramekin sides. Brush melted butter over parchment paper and cover ramekins. Bake until mousse is set and begins to pull away from sides, about 20 minutes. Remove from oven and tip each ramekin onto its side to drain excess cooking liquid. Run a knife around the edges and invert each mousse onto a plate.

Arrange a piece of smoked salmon over the top of each mousse and garnish with dill sprigs.

1 tbs unsalted butter, softened, plus 3 tbs butter, melted

12 oz sole fillet, cut into ½-inch cubes, chilled

10 oz salmon fillet, skinless, cut into ½-inch cubes, chilled

⅓ cup shallots, minced

1 tsp fresh chives, chopped

1 tsp fresh Italian parsley, chopped

1 tsp fresh dill, chopped, plus sprigs for garnish

½ tsp freshly ground pepper

3 large egg whites, chilled

1 cup heavy cream, chilled

8 slices smoked salmon

Kosher salt

DINNER

Honoring His Excellency
The Prime Minister of the Republic of Poland

Cucumber Mousse & Smoked Salmon
Caviar Sauce
Fleurons

Châteaubriand Jardinière
Sauce Foyot
Potatoes Dauphine

Kentucky Bibb Lettuce
Garden Herb Dressing
Saga Blue & Vermont Cheddar

Délice Gianduja
Bitter Orange Sauce

STAG'S LEAP WINE CELLARS Chardonnay Reserve 1986
YORK MOUNTAIN Pinot Noir Reserve 1987
ESSENSIA California Orange Muscat 1987

THE WHITE HOUSE
Wednesday, March 21, 1990

The State Dining Room set up for the Prime Minister of Poland. Raspberry colored tablecloths and Johnson china were used.

When everyone has finished dinner, the President and First Lady lead their guests out of the dining room, down the cross-hall where the Army Strolling Strings are playing, and into the Blue Room, where coffee is served. Coffee is also served in the Red and Green rooms. Here the Bushes are escorting Prime Minister Mazawiecki of Poland into the Blue Room.

Chateaubriand Jardinière

Serves 6

Rinse beef, pat dry, sprinkle with salt and pepper, and place in a large bowl.

In a small bowl, whisk together wine, brandy, onion, thyme, and bay leaf. Pour over beef, cover, and marinate for 24 hours, turning occasionally.

The next day, preheat oven to 425°F.

Remove beef from refrigerator and bring to room temperature. Place beef in a roasting pan, setting marinade aside, and roast in oven for 50–60 minutes for medium rare (145°F on a meat thermometer). Baste frequently with pan juices and marinade. Remove from oven and let rest for 20 minutes before slicing.

5 lb beef tenderloin

1 cup red wine

½ cup brandy

½ cup yellow onion, chopped

½ teaspoon fresh thyme leaves

1 bay leaf

Kosher salt

Freshly ground black pepper

Potatoes Dauphine

Serves 6

Peel and cut potatoes into quarters and boil until soft. Process potatoes through a ricer, or mash. (There should be about 2 cups).

In a saucepan, combine ½ cup water, butter, nutmeg, a sprinkle of salt and pepper, and bring to a boil. Stir in flour, reduce heat to medium, and beat vigorously with a wooden spoon for 3 minutes, or until paste pulls away from side of pan and forms a ball.

Remove from heat and add eggs 1 at a time, beating after each addition until smooth and shiny. Add potatoes and continue beating until combined.

In a deep fryer or large, deep pot, heat 2 inches of oil to 340°F on a deep-fat thermometer. Shape mixture into 1-inch balls—by hand or with a melon baller, then drop in hot oil and fry, turning with a slotted spoon, for 3 minutes. Once crisp and golden, transfer onto paper towels to drain, and sprinkle with salt.

Continue in batches until all batter has been used. Serve immediately, or place on baking sheets to keep warm in a 250°F oven.

1½ lbs russet potatoes

3 tbs unsalted butter

Pinch of freshly grated nutmeg

½ cup all-purpose flour

2 large eggs

Vegetable oil for deep-frying

Kosher salt

Freshly ground black pepper

April 26, 1990

DINNER
Honoring His Excellency
The President of the Republic of Venezuela
and Mrs. Perez

Smoked Trout & Asparagus Mousse
Horseradish Chantilly
Sesame Twists

Suprême of Duckling à l'Orange
Wild Rice Amandine
Belgian Endive & Sugar Peas

Spring Salad
Olive Oil & Herb Dressing
Saint Paulin Cheese

Spring Bombe
Sabayon Sauce
Cookies

MATANZAS CREEK Chardonnay 1988
SAINTSBURY Pinot Noir 1988
GABRIELE Y CAROLINE Riesling 1982

THE WHITE HOUSE
Thursday, April 26, 1990

I always made my own last-minute check that everything was in perfect order prior to each State Dinner. With the help of two Social Asides, I am checking the place cards at each table in the State Dining Room.

Suprême of Duckling à l'Orange

Serves 4

Using a sharp knife, score skin side of duck breasts in 2 directions, about 20 slashes per direction. Season generously on both sides with salt and pepper, cover, and refrigerate.

Use a knife or zesting tool to cut 4—2-inch strips of zest from oranges. Cut zest into a fine julienne and blanch for 1 minute in boiling water. Juice oranges, strain juice into a saucepan, and boil until reduced to about 2 tablespoons.

Heat a heavy skillet over medium heat and sauté duck, skin side down, 8–10 minutes. Turn over, increase heat to high, and cook for 1 more minute. Remove and set aside.

Discard fat and add reduced orange juice to deglaze skillet. Using a whisk, add stock, sugar, Grand Marnier, orange zest, and vinegar. Simmer for 1 minute to cook off alcohol, then whisk in butter, keeping whisk moving until melted. Season with salt and pepper, and if desired, add a few more drops of vinegar.

Slice duck breasts crosswise and arrange on individual plates. Spoon sauce over the top and serve with orange slices on the side.

4 Pekin duck breasts

2 juicing oranges

1 cup water, boiling

2 tbs olive oil

1 cup chicken stock

¼ tsp sugar

2 tbs Grand Marnier

2 tbs red wine vinegar

3 tbs unsalted butter, cold

Kosher salt

Freshly ground black pepper

Orange slices for garnish

Wild Rice Amandine

Serves 4

Preheat oven to 325°F.

In a large saucepan, heat olive oil and sauté onion and shallot until translucent. Stir in chives then add rice, and cook for 1 minute, stirring constantly. Add stock and almonds, and season with salt and pepper. Transfer to a casserole dish and bake, covered, for 60–75 minutes, until rice is tender, stirring once or twice while baking.

1 tbs extra virgin olive oil

2 tbs yellow onion, chopped

1 tsp shallot, minced

2 tbs chives, chopped

2 cups wild rice, rinsed well

4½ cups chicken stock

¾ cup almonds, slivered

Kosher salt

Freshly ground black pepper

May 15, 1990

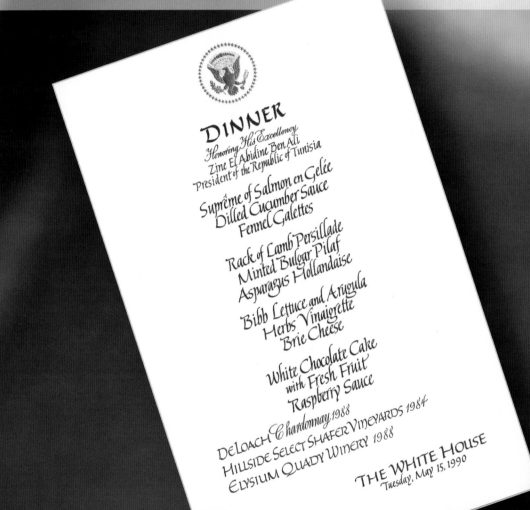

DINNER

Honoring His Excellency
Zine El Abidine Ben Ali
President of the Republic of Tunisia

Suprême of Salmon en Gelée
Dilled Cucumber Sauce
Fennel Galettes

Rack of Lamb Persillade
Minted Bulgar Pilaf
Asparagus Hollandaise

Bibb Lettuce and Arugula
Herbs Vinaigrette
Brie Cheese

White Chocolate Cake
with Fresh Fruit
Raspberry Sauce

DeLoach Chardonnay 1988
Hillside Select Shafer Vineyards 1984
Elysium Quady Winery 1988

THE WHITE HOUSE
Tuesday, May 15, 1990

Just before guests arrive, the waiters meet and make their final table check. It goes without saying that these waiters are the very best. Many of them have served the White House as long as 40 years…through nine and ten presidents.

Rack of Lamb Persillade

Serves 6

Preheat oven to 450°F.

Rinse lamb, pat dry, remove excess fat, and rub with olive oil then season with salt and pepper. Place in roasting pan with fat side up and roast in oven for 10 minutes.

While lamb is roasting, process garlic, parsley, and rosemary in a food processor until well combined and finely minced. Add breadcrumbs and lemon zest and pulse a couple more times until combined.

Remove lamb and cover with breadcrumb mixture, pressing so it sticks. Drizzle melted butter over top and return to oven for 15 more minutes, or until meat thermometer registers 130°F–140°F for medium rare.

Remove from oven and let rest for 15 minutes before slicing to serve.

2 large racks of lamb (6 bones each), frenched

2 tbs extra virgin olive oil

3 garlic cloves, peeled

2 cups fresh Italian parsley, chopped

2 tbs fresh rosemary, chopped

1 cup breadcrumbs

2 tsp lemon zest

¼ cup unsalted butter, melted

Kosher salt

Freshly ground black pepper

White Chocolate Cake with Fresh Fruit

Preheat oven to 350°F.

Sift flour, baking soda, baking powder, and salt together. Set aside.

In a small saucepan, melt white chocolate in hot water over low heat. Stir until smooth, and cool to room temperature.

In a large mixing bowl, cream butter and sugar until light and fluffy. Add eggs one at a time, beating thoroughly with each addition. Stir in flour mixture, buttermilk, and chocolate.

Pour batter into two 9-inch round cake pans and bake for 30–35 minutes until a toothpick inserted into the center comes out clean. Remove and cool on racks.

While cake is cooling, make frosting. In a medium bowl, combine white chocolate, flour, and milk. Cook over medium heat, stirring constantly, until very thick. Cool completely.

In large mixing bowl, beat butter, sugar, and vanilla until light and fluffy. Gradually add cooled chocolate and beat at high speed until it is the consistency of whipped cream.

Remove cake from pans and spread ⅓ of frosting on one cake, place second cake on top and spread remaining frosting over top and around sides. Serve with fresh seasonal fruit.

White Chocolate Cake

2½ cups all-purpose flour

1 tsp baking soda

½ tsp baking powder

½ tsp salt

6 oz white chocolate, chopped

½ cup hot water

1 cup unsalted butter, room temperature

1½ cups sugar

2 tsp vanilla

3 eggs

1 cup buttermilk

Frosting

6 oz white chocolate, chopped

2½ tbs all-purpose flour

1 cup milk

1 cup unsalted butter, softened

1 cup sugar

1 tsp vanilla extract

Fresh seasonal fruit

Asparagus Hollandaise

Serves 6

Break off ends of asparagus and rinse under cold water. If desired, peel skin on lower part of stalks.

Add salt to a deep pot and bring 2–3 inches of water to a boil. Tie a string around asparagus and stand them upright in pot. Cover, and boil for 15–18 minutes, until asparagus is tender.

Drain, and arrange on a serving platter.

Hollandaise Sauce
Heat a small saucepan over very low heat and add egg yolks and lemon juice stirring with a wooden spoon. Add butter one tablespoon at a time, stirring until melted. Continue to stir over low heat until sauce thickens, being careful not to cook too quickly or too high or sauce will curdle.

Pour Hollandaise Sauce over asparagus before serving. Garnish with lemon zest if desired.

Asparagus
2 lbs asparagus
1 tsp kosher salt

Hollandaise Sauce
2 large egg yolks
3 tbs fresh lemon juice
½ cup unsalted butter

May 31, 1990

Dinner

*Honoring His Excellency
The President of
the Union of Soviet Socialist Republics
and Mrs. Gorbachev*

Maine Lobster en Gelée
Aurora Sauce
Corn Sticks

Roasted Filet of Beef Mascotte
Green Peppercorn Sauce
Asparagus, Sauce Aveline

Mixed Spring Salad
Lemon & Olive Oil Dressing
Saint Paulin Cheese

Lime Turban with Iced Raspberries
Friandises

FLORA SPRINGS *Barrel Fermented Chardonnay 1987*
HEITZ CELLARS MARTHA'S *Cabernet Sauvignon 1974*
VINEYARD
S. ANDERSON *Blanc de Noirs Cuvée Extraordinaire 1985*

THE WHITE HOUSE
Thursday, May 31, 1990

The Bushes and the Gorbechevs coming down the Grand Stairway at their State Dinner. The Honor Guard leads the way, and at the bottom of the stairs the Marine Orchestra plays "Hail to the Chief."

A State Dinner table setting using the Johnson China, my personal favorite, depicts wild flowers from all over the United States. There are only 160 place settings—some have been lost through breakage over the years.

Roasted Fillet of Beef Mascotte with Green Peppercorn Sauce

Serves 8

Preheat oven to 350°F.

Rinse tenderloin and pat dry. In a small bowl, combine garlic, rosemary, and mustard and season with salt and pepper. Thoroughly rub mixture into tenderloin until completely covered.

Heat olive oil in a large roasting pan over high and brown tenderloin on all sides, 2–3 minutes per side.

Drain artichokes and add them to roasting pan. Roast on middle oven rack until meat thermometer registers 120°F, 25–30 minutes.

Remove tenderloin from pan, place on a cutting board, and let rest for 15 minutes before slicing. Remove artichokes from pan and set aside. While tenderloin rests, make Green Peppercorn Sauce (p. 58) in the same pan.

Serve tenderloin with artichokes on the side and sauce drizzled over the top.

4 lb beef tenderloin, trimmed and tied

2 garlic cloves, minced

¼ cup fresh rosemary, chopped

2 tbs coarse Dijon mustard

¼ cup extra virgin olive oil

1 (14 oz) can artichoke hearts (not marinated)

Kosher salt

Freshly ground black pepper

Green Peppercorn Sauce

Melt butter in same roasting pan as beef tenderloin (p. 56) then add shallots and sauté 2–3 minutes, stirring. Add peppercorns, cream, mustard and tarragon. Bring to a boil, stirring, until large, shiny bubbles form and sauce is slightly thickened, about 3–4 minutes. Stir in accumulated juices from cutting board where beef is resting and season with salt and pepper.

1 tbs unsalted butter

½ cup shallots, minced

2 tbs green peppercorns, rinsed and drained

¾ cup whipping cream

1 tbs coarse Dijon mustard

1 tbs dry tarragon

Kosher salt

Freshly ground black pepper

Corn Sticks

Makes 18 sticks

Preheat oven to 425°F.

Sift flour, sugar, baking powder, and salt together in a large bowl. Stir in cornmeal. In a small bowl, combine egg, corn, milk, and oil, then add to dry ingredients. Stir until dry ingredients are moist.

Heat cast iron corn stick pans or jelly roll pan for 5–7 minutes in oven, then remove and grease generously. Fill pans 2/3 full and bake for 20 minutes.

Remove and invert corn stick pans so that corn sticks fall out, or if using a jelly roll pan, remove and slice into even "sticks."

1 cup all-purpose flour

2 tbs sugar

2 tsp baking powder

¾ tsp salt

1 cup yellow cornmeal

1 egg, beaten

8 oz canned creamed corn

¾ cup whole milk

2 tbs vegetable oil

July 10, 1990

DINNER

1990 ECONOMIC SUMMIT
of INDUSTRIALIZED NATIONS

Chilled Yellow Tomato Soup
with Avocado Relish

Hickory Grilled Veal Loin Medallions
with Morel Sauce
Sweet Corn Pudding
Haricots Vert, Julienne Carrots
& Julienne Red Bell Pepper

Texas Lettuces with Walnut Vinaigrette
American Cheeses

Cobbler of Cherokee Blackberries
and Texas Peaches
with Sweetened Cream

LLANO ESTACADO Chardonnay 1987
SAINTSBURY Pinot Noir 1988
RENAISSANCE Special Select Late Harvest White Riesling 1985

THE MUSEUM OF FINE ARTS
Houston, Texas · Tuesday, July 10, 1990

60

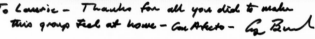

To Laurie — Thanks for all you did to make this group feel at home — Con Atheto — Gy Bush

In 1990, the president hosted the G-7 Economic Summit at Rice University in Houston, Texas. The leaders and their spouses from Great Britain, France, Germany, Italy, Canada, Japan, and the European Union meet annually, rotating the host country. For three days, the President entertained the seven heads of state at breakfast, lunch, and dinner.

President Bush, Secretary of State Jim Baker, and me in the suite at the Waldorf Astoria Hotel after meetings with the heads of State during a United Nations Assembly meeting in New York.

Chilled Yellow Tomato Soup with Avocado Relish

Serves 4

Rinse tomatoes and slice in quarters, removing core and seeds.

Heat olive oil in a sauce pan over medium heat. Add shallots and sauté for 2–3 minutes then add tomatoes and thyme and season with salt. Simmer for 30 minutes, remove from heat, and let cool slightly before placing in a blender to purée until smooth. Strain through a fine mesh sieve then stir in cream and season with salt. Chill in refrigerator for at least 30 minutes.

Avocado Relish
Slice avocado in half, discard pit and skin and place flesh in a bowl. Add onion, jalapeño, lime juice, and cilantro and mash with a potato masher. Season to taste with salt and pepper.

To serve, ladle soup into bowls and place a dollop of Avocado Relish on top.

Yellow Tomato Soup

4 large yellow tomatoes

¼ cup extra virgin olive oil

2 shallots, sliced

2 fresh thyme sprigs, leaves removed

1 cup heavy cream

Kosher salt

Avocado Relish

1 ripe Haas avocado

1 tbs red onion, diced

1 tsp jalapeño pepper, minced

2 tbs fresh lime juice

Hickory Grilled Veal Loin Medallions with Morel Sauce

Serves 4

Place veal in a shallow baking dish and season with salt and pepper. Combine olive oil, lemon juice, vinegar, garlic, and rosemary in a small bowl and pour over veal. Marinate in refrigerator for a minimum 1 hour, up to overnight.

Remove veal from refrigerator and bring to room temperature. Heat a grill and place hickory chips according to package directions depending on if grill is gas or charcoal. Grill for 5–7 minutes on each side. Remove, and let rest for 10 minutes.

Morel Sauce
Boil water and sugar in a small saucepan until golden caramel. Remove from heat and slowly add red-wine and balsamic vinegar down side of pan (mixture will bubble and steam). Return to heat and stir until caramel dissolves, about 3 minutes, then remove from heat again.

In a heavy saucepan, melt butter and sauté morels, stirring, until liquid has evaporated, about 5 minutes. Transfer morels with slotted spoon to a bowl and set aside. Add shallots to pan and sauté, stirring, until golden. Add wine and boil until reduced to 1 cup, about 15 minutes, then add stock and reserved morel liquid (if using dried morels), and reduce to 1¼ cups, about 15 more minutes.

Remove from heat and stir in caramel mixture. Add morels and season with salt and pepper. If desired add additional balsamic vinegar and lemon juice.

Drizzle Morel Sauce over Veal Medallions.

Veal Medallions

4 (8 oz) veal loin chops

2 tbs extra virgin olive oil

3 tbs fresh lemon juice

2 tbs balsamic vinegar

3 garlic cloves, minced

1 tbs fresh rosemary, chopped

Kosher salt

Freshly ground black pepper

Hickory chips for the grill

Morel Sauce

¼ cup water

¼ cup sugar

¼ cup red wine vinegar

1 tbs balsamic vinegar

3 tbs unsalted butter

16 oz fresh morel mushrooms, rinsed, patted dry, and trimmed, or 1 ounce dried morels, soaked, reserving ½ cup soaking liquid

⅓ cup shallots, minced

2 cups dry red wine

2 cups veal stock

Fresh lemon juice to taste

Sweet Corn Pudding

Serves 4

Preheat oven to 350°F.

Butter 4 (16 oz) ramekins. Place all ingredients in a food processor with a steel blade and process until almost smooth. Pour batter into prepared ramekins and bake until brown and center is just set, about 45 minutes. Cool for 10 minutes before serving.

2 cups fresh or frozen corn kernels

2 tbs unsalted butter, room temperature

2 large eggs

1 tbs all-purpose flour

½ cup whipping cream

1 tsp baking powder

¼ cup whole milk

½ tsp Kosher salt

3 tbs sugar

Cobbler of Cherokee Blackberries and Texas Peaches with Sweetened Cream

Serves 8

Preheat oven to 350°F.

Pit and peel peaches then cut into 1-inch slices. Combine peaches, cornstarch, sugar, and lemon juice in a large bowl, tossing gently. Carefully fold in blackberries and transfer to a baking dish.

Topping
In a mixer fitted with a paddle attachment, combine flour, salt, brown sugar, baking powder, cinnamon, and nutmeg. Add butter, 1 tablespoon at a time, and mix until crumbly. Add ¾ cup of milk and continue mixing until just combined. Break off balls of dough and place them on top of fruit.

Brush top of dough with remaining milk and sprinkle with sugar. Place cobbler on a sheet-pan to catch any juices that spill over and bake for 25–30 minutes, until top is golden brown and juices are bubbling. Serve warm or at room temperature with a dollop of Sweetened Cream.

Sweetened Cream
Beat whipping cream with a mixer at high speed until extremely thick. Add sugar and vanilla until combined. Serve with cobbler.

10 yellow peaches

1 tbs cornstarch

¼ cup light brown sugar

2 tsp fresh lemon juice

2 cups blackberries

Topping

2 cups flour

½ tsp salt

¼ cup light brown sugar, packed

2 tsp baking powder

¼ tsp cinnamon

2 pinches freshly grated nutmeg

6 tbs cold, unsalted butter

¾ cup plus 1 tbs milk

1 tbs sugar

Sweetened Cream

¾ cup whipping cream

1 tbs powdered sugar

1 tsp vanilla extract

DINNER
Honoring
Her Majesty Queen Elizabeth II
and
His Royal Highness The Prince Philip
Duke of Edinburgh

Médaillons of Maine Lobster and Cucumber Mousse
Aurora Sauce
Galettes Fines Herbes

Crown Roast of Lamb
Dauphine Potatoes
Bouquettes of Vegetables

Watercress and Belgian Endive Salad
St. Andre and Chevre Cheese

Pistachio Marquise with
Fresh Raspberries

SWANSON Reserve Chardonnay 1988
SHAFER HILLSIDE Select Cabernet Sauvignon 1986
JORDAN, J 1987

THE WHITE HOUSE
Tuesday, May 14, 1991

This is the West-End sitting room in the family quarters on the second floor. Here I was introduced to Queen Elizabeth in her famous hat.

When the Queen was making her remarks at the arrival ceremony on the South lawn during her State Visit, the aide neglected to pull out the step behind the podium to bring her to the correct height behind the microphone. Being a true Queen, she never said anything at the time and carried on as if nothing were wrong.

Crown Roast of Lamb

Serves 6

In a food processor, fitted with a metal blade, combine mustard, butter, onions, garlic, rosemary, parsley, and lemon juice until they form a paste. Generously season lamb with salt and pepper then rub paste into lamb, covering all sides. Wrap lamb tightly with plastic wrap and refrigerate overnight.

The next day, preheat oven to 400°F.

Remove lamb from refrigerator and bring to room temperature. Place in a roasting pan and roast for 30–35 minutes or, until a meat thermometer reads 135°F for medium rare. Remove, and let rest for 15 minutes before slicing.

1 cup grainy Dijon mustard

½ cup unsalted butter, room temperature

½ cup yellow onions, chopped

3 garlic cloves, peeled

2 tbs fresh rosemary, chopped

¼ cup fresh Italian parsley leaves, chopped

2 tbs fresh lemon juice

5 lb crown roast of lamb

Kosher salt

Freshly ground black pepper

Watercress and Belgian Endive Salad

Serves 6

Whisk together vinegar, mustard, garlic, sea salt, and pepper in a bowl until salt has dissolved. Add oil in a slow stream, whisking until emulsified.

Rinse watercress, pat dry, and discard coarse stems. Rinse endive, dry, and separate leaves. Slice radishes.

Toss watercress, endive, and radishes in a large bowl, coating with just enough dressing, and season with salt and pepper.

3 tsp white wine vinegar

¾ cup Dijon mustard

1 garlic clove, minced

Pinch of sea salt

Pinch of freshly ground black pepper

¼ cup extra virgin olive oil

2 large bunches watercress or mixed greens

2–3 Belgian endives, green or red

3–4 radishes

Luncheon
Honoring
The Ladies of the Senate

Purée of Minted Melon
Soup Macaroons

Champagne Poached Salmon en Gelée
Sauce Verte

Summer Vegetable Vinaigrette
Galettes Fines Herbes

Lime Mousse with Fresh Cherries
Cookies

FERRARI-CARANO
Chardonnay 1989

THE WHITE HOUSE
Wednesday June 12, 1991

The annual Senate Ladies luncheon in the State Dining Room, was hosted by Mrs. Bush. The Senate Ladies began meeting during World War I to roll bandages for the troops. They continue to meet every Tuesday when Congress is in session to crochet blankets and make hand puppets for Children's Hospital.

This is Raggedy Ann and Andy, the Christmas ornaments that Mrs. Bush needlepointed for the tree. We later used some of the ornaments like this one as centerpieces for the Ladies lunches, because they were so unique and beautiful.

Purée of Minted Melon Soup

Serves 4

Purée cantaloupe and honeydew in a blender until smooth. Add lime juice, lemon juice, Champagne, mint, and honey, and purée until thoroughly combined. Pour into a pitcher, cover, and refrigerate at least 1 hour, until well chilled.

Pour melon soup into bowls and garnish with melon balls, raspberries, and lime zest.

1 cantaloupe, cut into chunks

½ honeydew melon, cut into chunks

2 tbs fresh lime juice

3 tbs fresh lemon juice

¼ cup Champagne or sparkling wine

1 tbs fresh mint, chopped

1 tbs honey

¼ cup plain yogurt

8 raspberries

Lime zest

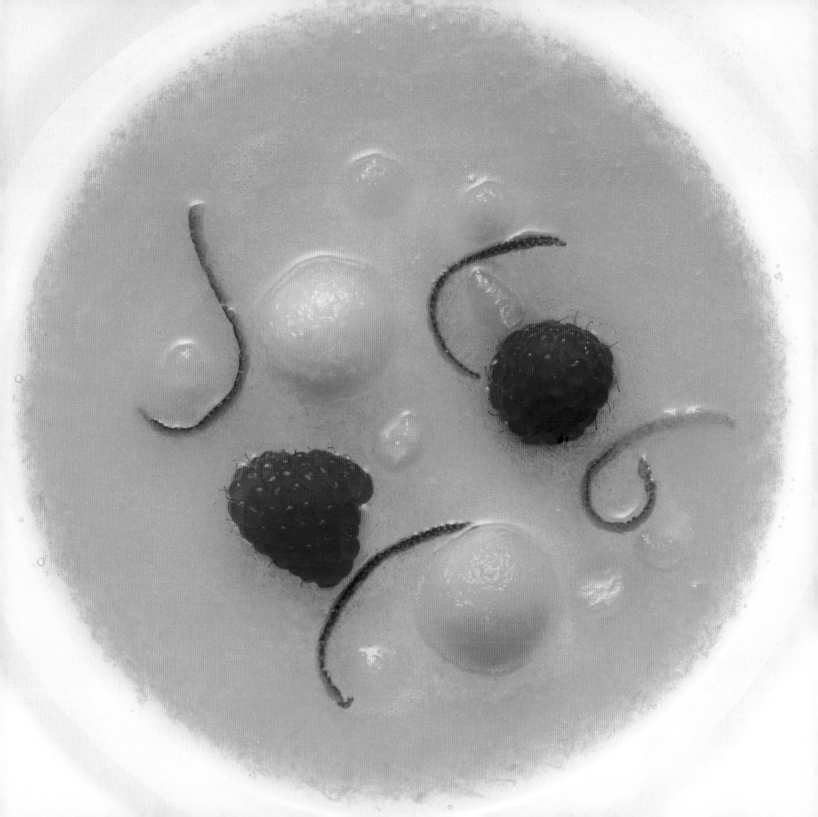

Champagne Poached Salmon en Gelée

Serves 4

Rinse salmon, pat dry, and season with salt and pepper. Pour champagne and lime juice into a large, flat pan, and bring to a boil. Add salmon (if necessary, add a little water to cover completely), and place onions, tarragon sprigs, and capers over the top. Bring liquid to a gentle simmer and cover to poach for 6 minutes, being careful that liquid does not boil.

While salmon is poaching, combine mustard and chopped tarragon in a small bowl seasoning with salt and pepper to taste.

Once salmon is poached, discard liquid and arrange on a platter. Garnish with chives and lemon slices, serving tarragon mustard sauce on the side.

2 lb salmon fillet

2 cups Champagne or sparkling wine

¼ cup fresh lime juice

4 red onion slices

4 fresh tarragon sprigs, plus 2 tsp, chopped

1 tbs capers, drained

½ cup Dijon mustard

Kosher or sea salt

Freshly ground pepper

Fresh chives

Lemon slices

Lime Mousse with Fresh Cherries

Serves 4

In a sauce pan, dissolve gelatin in warm water over low heat stirring until all lumps are gone.

In a bowl, combine gelatin, lime zest, and lime juice, stirring well. Add sugar and yogurt, stirring until combined. Beat egg whites until soft peaks form, adding cream of tarter and a few drops of lime juice to stabilize, then fold into lime mixture.

Pour into 4 individual ramekins dishes, cover with plastic wrap, and refrigerate for a minimum of 4 hours before serving, until well chilled.

Before serving, soak ramekins in a warm water bath for a few minutes and cut around mousse with a thin knife. Invert onto individual dishes and garnish with cherries and mint.

¼ oz envelope unflavored powdered gelatin

¼ cup warm water

1 tbs lime zest

½ cup fresh lime juice, strained

¼ cup sugar

1 cup low fat vanilla yogurt

3 egg whites, room temperature

Pinch of cream of tartar

8–10 fresh cherries, pitted

Mint sprigs

June 18, 1991

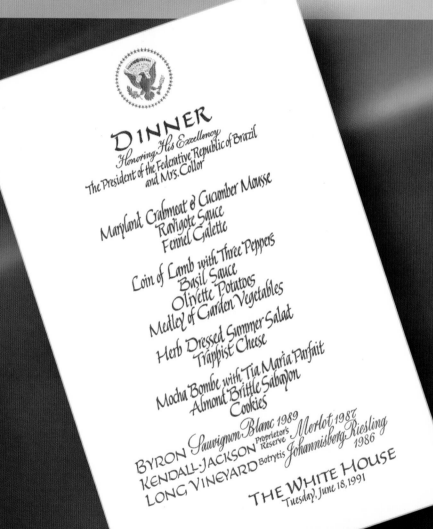

DINNER

Honoring His Excellency
The President of the Federative Republic of Brazil
and Mrs. Collor

Maryland Crabmeat & Cucumber Mousse
Ravigote Sauce
Fennel Galette

Loin of Lamb with Three Peppers
Basil Sauce
Olivette Potatoes
Medley of Garden Vegetables

Herb Dressed Summer Salad
Trappist Cheese

Mocha Bombe with Tia Maria Parfait
Almond Brittle Sabayon
Cookies

Byron Sauvignon Blanc 1989
Kendall-Jackson Proprietor's Reserve Merlot 1987
Long Vineyard Botrytis Johannisberg Riesling 1986

THE WHITE HOUSE
Tuesday, June 18, 1991

This is the First Ladies Garden on the southeast side of the White House. We often had a small buffet for guests here before showing them a movie.

This is the movie theater, which is on the ground floor. Showing movies was usually an impromptu evening, sometimes with dinner before, but always informal and relaxed with popcorn and sodas.

Loin of Lamb with Three Peppers

Serves 4

Preheat oven to 350°F.

Rinse lamb and pat dry, rub with 1 tablespoon of olive oil and season with salt.

In a bowl, combine remaining olive oil, basil, parsley, garlic, and pepper to form a paste. Rub thoroughly into lamb.

Heat an ovenproof skillet over medium and sear lamb on all sides until lightly browned, 2–3 minutes per side. Place skillet in oven and roast until lamb is medium rare, 10–15 minutes. Remove, cover with foil, and let rest for 15 minutes.

While lamb is resting, make basil sauce to serve on the side.

Basil Sauce
Add garlic, basil, and salt in a food processor and process until they form a paste. While food processor is running, add olive oil a little at a time until emulsified and season with salt and pepper.

Lamb Loin

3 lb lamb tenderloin, trimmed and tied

2 tbs extra virgin olive oil, separated

1 tbs fresh basil, chopped

1 tbs fresh Italian parsley, chopped

2 garlic cloves, minced

2 tsp freshly ground 3-pepper blend

Kosher salt

Basil Sauce

4 garlic cloves, peeled

4 cups fresh basil leaves

¼ tsp Kosher salt

⅓ cup extra virgin olive oil

Luncheon

*Honoring His Excellency
The President of
The Union of Soviet Socialist Republics*

Chilled Vichyssoise
with Beluga Caviar

Noisettes of Lamb with Lemon Thyme
Baby Potatoes
Mixed Spring Vegetables

White Chocolate & Passion Fruit Mousse
Vanilla Anglaise Sauce

SWANSON
Chardonnay 1988

ACACIA
Cabernet Sauvignon 1984

WINFIELD HOUSE
LONDON, ENGLAND
Wednesday, July 17, 1991

After the signing ceremony, the two Presidents held a press conference in the Rose Garden. In addition to the strategic arms reduction agreement, the Presidents agreed to work together to develop a concept for global protection systems against limited ballistic missile attacks.

Mrs. Bush hosts a luncheon on the front porch of George Washington's home, Mount Vernon, for Mrs. Yeltsin, while the Yeltsin's were in the US on their State visit. Mrs. Yeltsin is toasting Mrs. Bush.

Chilled Vichyssoise with Beluga Caviar

Serves 4

Simmer potatoes and leeks in stock until tender. Transfer to a blender and purée until smooth. Add cream and season to taste with salt and pepper. Cover, and chill in the refrigerator.

Serve in chilled soup bowls and garnish with chives and caviar.

1½ cups Idaho potatoes, peeled and sliced into quarters

1½ cups leeks, sliced, white parts only

3 cups chicken stock

¼ cup heavy whipping cream

Fresh chives

Kosher salt

Freshly ground white pepper

Beluga caviar

Noisettes of Lamb with Lemon Thyme

Serves 4

Rinse lamb and pat dry. In a bowl, combine 2 tablespoons olive oil, thyme, garlic, and breadcrumbs, then thoroughly rub into lamb.

Heat remaining olive oil in heavy pan. Once oil is hot, sear lamb for 5–7 minutes on each side, or until meat thermometer registers 145°F for medium-rare. Remove and let rest for 10 minutes before serving. Slice, and if desired, sprinkle additional minced thyme and squeeze lemon juice over lamb.

2 lb lamb tenderloin

3 tbs extra virgin olive oil, separated

2 tbs lemon thyme, minced

2 garlic cloves, minced

¼ cup breadcrumbs

Kosher salt

Freshly ground black pepper

White Chocolate and Passion Fruit Mousse

Serves 4

Break chocolate into small pieces and melt in a double boiler or microwave. Set aside and let cool.

Beat egg whites in a large bowl until stiff. Add egg yolks to cooled chocolate and stir gently to combine.

Slice passion fruit in half and scoop juice, pulp, and seeds into chocolate, then fold into egg whites until thoroughly combined.

Place raspberries in the bottom of a glass bowl or trifle dish. Pour mousse into bowl, cover, and chill in the refrigerator for at least 4 hours. Sprinkle peanuts on the top before serving.

5 oz white chocolate

3 large eggs, separated

5 passion-fruits

½ lb raspberries (fresh or frozen)

2 tbs peanuts, chopped

July 31, 1991

DINNER

Honoring His Excellency
The President of the
Union of Soviet Socialist Republics
and Mrs. Gorbachev

Watercress Soup
Sesame Twists

Roast Tenderloin of Beef, Truffle Sauce
Tiny Roasted Potatoes
Haricots Verts & Baby Carrots

Mixed Green Salad
Herb Dressing
Trappist & Brie Cheese

Lime Sorbet with Vodka Mousse
Fresh Raspberries Sabayon
Cookies

Cuvaison Chardonnay 1990
Beaulieu Vineyards Georges de Latour Cabernet Sauvignon 1970
PRIVATE RESERVE
Iron Horse Brut "Summit Cuvée" 1987

SPASO HOUSE
MOSCOW
Wednesday, July 31, 1991

We held a reciprocal dinner during our visit to Moscow, in which the Bushes hosted a dinner at Spaso house, our Ambassador's residence. Hans Raffert, the White House Chef, flew over with the food and china. Pictured here are the Gorbachevs and the U.S. Ambassador Jack Matlock and his wife with President and Mrs. Bush.

President Bush is introducing me to President Gorbachev during the dinner at Spaso House, the U.S. Ambassador's residence in Moscow.

95

Watercress Soup

Serves 6

Heat olive oil in a heavy saucepan and sauté onions until translucent, about 3–5 minutes. Add watercress and stock and bring to a boil. Reduce heat and simmer for 15 minutes, until watercress is tender. Remove watercress and onion from stock and purée with ½ cup of stock in a blender until smooth. Return purée to stock, add lime juice, and sugar, and season with salt and pepper. Bring to a boil then simmer for 2–3 more minutes.

Serve with a garnish of watercress.

1 tbs extra virgin olive oil

½ cup onion, chopped

¼ lb watercress, roots trimmed

4 cups vegetable stock

2 tbs fresh lime juice

½ tsp sugar

Kosher salt

Freshly ground pepper

October 28, 1991

DINNER

Honoring Her Majesty
The Queen of Thailand

Lobster Bisque with Quenelles
Pesto Galettes

Crown Roast of Lamb
Château Potatoes
Acorn Squash, Baby Corn & Snow Peas

Autumn Salad
Almond Brie Cheese

Fruit Sorbets Surprise
with Sabayon Sauce
Petits Fours

Sanford Chardonnay 1989
Star Hill Pinot Noir 1988
Domain Chandon Brut

THE WHITE HOUSE
Monday, October 28, 1991

Dinner for Queen Sirkit of Thailand in the Family Dining Room on the second floor. The 18th century chandelier highlights the wallpaper, "The War of Independence," which Mrs. Kennedy had done when she converted the room from a bedroom into its present use as a dining room. The wallpaper was temporarily removed during the 1970's by the Ford Administration. President Carter re-installed it. The Clintons had it removed und upholstered the walls in pale green silk.

Lobster Bisque

Serves 4

Fill a large stock pot three-quarters full with salted water and bring to a boil. Plunge lobster headfirst into water and cook over high heat for 8 minutes, until red. Remove with tongs and place in a large bowl to cool. Reserve 2 cups of cooking liquid. Remove meat from lobster claws and tail, reserving juices, shells, and body. Coarsely chop meat and transfer to a bowl. Cover, and chill in refrigerator.

In a large stock pot, heat olive oil and sauté lobster shells and body, stirring occasionally, about 8 minutes. Add onion, celery, carrot, tomato, tarragon, thyme, bay leaf, peppercorns, and Sherry, and simmer, stirring, until almost all liquid has evaporated, about 5 minutes. Add stock and reserved lobster cooking liquid. Season with salt and pepper and simmer, uncovered, stirring occasionally, for 1 hour.

Pour stock through a fine sieve into a large saucepan, pressing on and discarding all solids. Whisk in tomato paste and simmer until reduced to 3 cups, about 10 minutes. Add cream and simmer for 5 minutes. In a small bowl, combine cornstarch and lobster juices then whisk into bisque. Simmer, stirring, for 2 minutes, then add lobster meat and simmer for 1 more minute and season with salt and pepper before serving.

Add croutons and chives as a garnish if desired.

3 lb live lobster

2 tbs extra virgin olive oil

1 yellow onion, quartered

1 celery stalk, quartered

1 carrot, quartered

1 tomato, seeds removed, quartered

2 fresh tarragon sprigs

3 fresh thyme sprigs

1 bay leaf

6 black peppercorns

½ cup dry Sherry

4 cups fish stock

¼ cup tomato paste

½ cup heavy cream

1 tsp cornstarch

Kosher or sea salt

Freshly ground pepper

LUNCHEON

Honoring
The Spouses of the Governors
of the States and Territories

Beef Consommé with Orzo
Melba Toast

Suprême of Red Snapper in Champagne
Fleurons
Purée of Carrots & Haricots Verts

Belgian Endive, Red Oak & Boston Lettuce

Gingerbread Soufflé

BOYER
Chardonnay 1990

THE WHITE HOUSE
Monday, February 3, 1992

A working lunch that President Bush hosted for French President Mitterand in a private home in Ocean Reef, Florida. Some events did not come off perfectly! Here, the Secret Service closed the curtain during lunch, blocking the panoramic view of the ocean, for security reasons!

Beef Consommé with Orzo

Serves 8

Heat butter and olive oil in a stockpot. Add onions, carrots, and celery and sauté 2–3 minutes. Add orzo and mushrooms and cook for 5 more minutes, stirring, then add broth and water, and bring to a boil. Reduce heat and simmer for 30 minutes until orzo is cooked. Season with salt and pepper and serve in soup bowls with chopped parsley.

2 tbs unsalted butter

2 tbs extra virgin olive oil

½ cup onions, diced

¼ cup carrots, diced

¼ cup celery, diced

2 cups orzo

1 cup sliced mushrooms

2½ cups condensed beef broth

1 cup water

2 tbs fresh Italian parsley, chopped

Kosher salt

Freshly ground pepper

Purée of Carrots and Haricots Verts

Serves 8

Carrot Purée
Melt butter in a heavy pan and add carrots. Sauté until tender then add cream, crème fraîche, ginger, and thyme and season with salt and pepper. Pour into a blender and purée until smooth.

Haricot Vert Purée
Melt butter in a heavy pan and sauté onions and garlic 2–3 minutes. Add haricot verts and sauté until tender then add cream, crème fraîche, mint, and thyme and season with salt and pepper. Pour into a blender and purée until smooth.

If desired, place a dollop of crème fraîche in the center with a sprig of thyme before serving.

Carrot Purée

1 tbs unsalted butter

2 cups carrots, peeled and sliced

3 tbs heavy cream

3 tbs crème fraîche

1 tsp ground ginger

1 tsp fresh thyme leaves

Kosher salt

Freshly ground pepper

Haricot Vert Purée

1 tbs butter

½ cup onions, chopped

1 garlic clove, minced

2 cups haricot verts (fresh or frozen, thawed)

3 tbs heavy cream

3 tbs crème fraîche

2 tbs fresh mint leaves, chopped

1 tsp fresh thyme leaves

Kosher salt

Freshly ground pepper

Gingerbread Soufflé

Serves 8

Preheat oven to 375°F.

Prepare 8 (6 oz) ramekins with butter.

In a heavy saucepan, bring milk to a boil. Add ginger, remove from heat, cover, and steep for 30 minutes. Strain milk, discarding ginger, and set aside.

In a large bowl, whisk egg yolks and 6 tablespoons of sugar together. Add flour and continue mixing until combined. Slowly, add milk, whisking constantly to prevent curdling. Return mixture to saucepan and cook over medium heat, whisking until custard boils and thickens enough to coat back of a spoon, 2–3 minutes. Transfer to a large bowl, stir in pumpkin, and set aside.

Using whisk attachment on electric mixer, beat egg whites until foamy and slightly opaque. With mixer running, add remaining sugar, 1 tablespoon at a time, and beat until stiff. Fold ⅓ of egg whites into pumpkin mixture to lighten, then add to remaining egg whites, folding gently but thoroughly. Spoon batter into ramekins, filling almost to top and place in a large baking pan. Add hot water to baking pan so ramekins are sitting half in water. Bake on middle oven rack until soufflés have risen well above rim and tops are golden brown, about 25 minutes. Serve immediately.

1½ cups whole milk

1 tbs fresh ginger, grated

4 egg yolks

¾ cup sugar, separated

5 tbs all-purpose flour

1 cup canned pumpkin, packed

8 egg whites

Hans Raffert Recipes

Hans Raffert, White House Chef, and myself in the
State Dining Room before a reception.

Following the entertainment, there is dancing and Champagne in the Grand Foyer. It is interesting to note the visiting Head of State does not stay for this part of the evening.

I'm greeting French President Francois Mitterand, when he came to President Bush's dinner in Munich, during an Economic Summit.

Orange Cantaloupe Soup

10 servings

Place melon in blender with orange juice, honey, and a pinch of salt; purée. Pour in a large bowl and add Champagne and yogurt. Stir until smooth then cover and refrigerate for at least 1 hour, until chilled.

Whip cream until stiff and add cinnamon. Remove soup from refrigerator and pour into chilled bowls. Place a dollop of whipped cream on the top and garnish with melon balls and mint leaves.

6 cups cantaloupe, peeled and seeded, cut into 1-inch pieces

1 cup freshly squeezed orange juice

3 tbs honey

1 cup Champagne

1 cup plain yogurt

1 cup whipped cream

1 tsp ground cinnamon

Fresh mint leaves for garnish

Kosher salt

Potato Gnocchi

Serves 8–10

Boil potatoes in a large pot with salted water until tender. Drain well and dry in the oven; set aside to cool. Once cool, pass potatoes through a coarse sieve or ricer. Mix eggs, milk, and flour thoroughly, then add to potatoes and season with salt and pepper. Work mixture to obtain a firm dough. Hand roll into finger-sized pieces and cook in salted, boiling water for about 6 minutes. Drain well, and brown in hot butter. Serve on a dish, sprinkled with Parmesan cheese.

As an entrée, this dish is accompanied by a "coulis" of tomatoes flavored with fresh herbs.

2 lbs russet potatoes, peeled and diced

6 eggs

⅓ cup milk

⅔ cup flour

6 tbs unsalted butter

⅔ cup Parmesan cheese, grated

Kosher salt

Freshly ground pepper

Ground nutmeg

Mrs. Bush's High Fiber Bran Muffins

Makes 4½ dozen, 1½ oz each

Preheat oven to 375°F.

In a large bowl, mix flour, bran, baking powder, salt, orange rind, and raisins together. Add eggs, honey, milk, oil, and vanilla and stir until blended. Use a #20 scoop portion of batter in a nonstick or lightly greased muffin tin. Place in oven and bake for 20–25 minutes. Make plenty and freeze them!

5 cups unsifted whole wheat flour

7½ cups miller's bran (can be purchased in health food stores and most supermarkets)

2 tbs baking powder

1½ tsp salt

2 cups raisins

2 tsp grated orange rind

10 eggs

1½ cups honey

1 quart non-fat milk

⅔ cup safflower oil

1½ tsp pure vanilla extract

Watercress Mousse

12 servings

Soak gelatin leaves in cold water. Once soft, melt in ¼ cup of water over low heat. Once melted, place in blender with watercress, stock, Tabasco, lemon juice, mustard, and cognac; purée until very fine. Add egg whites and cream and season with salt and pepper. Add a drop of green food coloring if desired. Refrigerate until serving.

5 leaves of gelatin, soaked in cold water

1 bunch (4 oz) watercress

1 cup chicken stock

Dash of Tabasco®

1 lemon, juiced, and grated a bit

1 tsp mild mustard

1 tbs cognac

2 egg whites, beaten stiff

1 cup heavy cream, whipped

Kosher salt

Freshly ground white pepper

Trace of green food coloring

Smoked Salmon Mousse

12 servings

Velouté Sauce

In a double boiler, melt butter. Stir in flour and gradually add stock. Stir over low heat until thickened. Return to double boiler and simmer over boiling water 1 hour, stirring occasionally. Soak gelatin in wine then add to stock, stirring. Strain through a fine sieve and let sauce cool to room temperature, but do not chill before adding to the mousse.

Mousse

In a food processor, purée smoked salmon and add to velouté sauce. Blend well, place in a bowl, and fold in whipped cream. Season to taste with salt, pepper, Tabasco, L&P sauce, dry mustard, and lemon juice, Pour mousse into a deep crystal dish and let set covered in refrigerator overnight. Use your talent to decorate!

Velouté Sauce

2 tbs unsalted butter

2 tbs flour

2 cups fish or chicken stock

1 tbs gelatin

¼ cup dry white wine

Mousse

1 lb smoked salmon

1½ cup velouté sauce

1 cup whipped cream

Salt to taste

White pepper to taste

Tabasco® to taste

L&P sauce to taste

Dry mustard to taste

Lemon juice to taste

Index

Index

CREDITS

An Affair to Remember
Copyright © 2006 by Silverback Books, Inc.

All rights reserved. No part of this book
may be used or reproduced in any manner
whatsoever without the prior written
permission of the publisher.

Project management and editing: Lynda
Zuber Sassi

Design: Richard Garnas

Layout and production: Patty Holden

Food photography: StockFood; Getty Images,
page 35

Menu cards courtesy of Laurie G. Firestone

Candid Photos: David Valdez

Printed in China

ISBN: 1-59637-057-2